CARBOHYDRATES

CARBOHYDRATES

BY DR. ALVIN SILVERSTEIN, VIRGINIA SILVERSTEIN, AND ROBERT SILVERSTEIN

ILLUSTRATIONS BY ANNE CANEVARI GREEN
FOOD POWER!
THE MILLBROOK PRESS ■ BROOKFIELD, CONNECTICUT

Library of Congress Cataloging-in-Publication Data

Silverstein, Alvin.
Carbohydrates / by Alvin, Virginia, and Robert Silverstein;
illustrations by Anne Canevari Green.

p.   cm.—(Food power!)
Includes bibliographical references and index.
Summary: Examines the different kinds of carbohydrates, their
sources, and their role in nutrition.
ISBN 1-56294-207-7 (lib. bdg.)
1. Carbohydrates—Juvenile literature.   2. Carbohydrates in
the body—Juvenile literature.   [1. Carbohydrates.]   I. Silverstein,
Virginia B.   II. Silverstein, Robert A.   III. Green, Anne
Canevari, ill.   IV. Title.   V. Series: Silverstein, Alvin. Food power!
QP70.S56   1992
612.3'96—dc20   91-41245   CIP   AC

CONTENTS

YOUR BODY IS JUST LIKE A FACTORY

1. **FOOD** IS THE **FUEL** THAT KEEPS YOUR FACTORY RUNNING.

2. THE FACTORY USES MANY THINGS IN FOOD: **CARBOHYDRATES**, **FATS**, **PROTEINS**, **VITAMINS**, **MINERALS**, AND **WATER** (WHICH HELPS COOL THE FACTORY AND CARRY THINGS AROUND IT).

3. **CARBOHYDRATES** (SUGARS AND STARCHES) ARE THE FURNACE — THEY PROVIDE ENERGY.

4. **FATS** ARE THE STORAGE DEPARTMENT: THEY STORE ENERGY FROM FOOD AND ALSO CARRY VITAMINS AROUND THE FACTORY.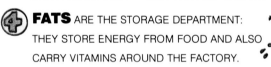

5. **PROTEINS** ARE THE BUILDING BLOCKS THAT ARE USED TO REPAIR AND ENLARGE THE FACTORY.

6. **VITAMINS** HELP TO RELEASE THE ENERGY FROM FATS, PROTEINS, AND CARBOHYDRATES.

7. **MINERALS** ARE THE CARPENTERS — THEY HELP TO BUILD BONES AND TEETH.

8. WHEN ALL FOOD IS COMPLETELY DIGESTED, WHATEVER ISN'T USED OR STORED LEAVES THE FACTORY AS **WASTE**.

GARBAGE

WHAT ARE CARBOHYDRATES?

Sugars and starches—are they good or bad for you? And what do they have in common?

Both sugars and starches belong to a chemical family called carbohydrates. Most fiber is a part of this group, too.

Sugars are the simplest of the carbohydrates. They are sweet and make foods taste good.

Starches are made of many sugar units linked together. They aren't sweet, but they help make a meal seem complete. (What would a sandwich be without the bread?)

Simple sugars are the building blocks for fiber, too. People have been talking a lot about fiber lately. Ads and TV commercials for cereals and breads brag about how much fiber they have and how good it is for you.

What's the real story about carbohydrates?

Carbohydrates are one of the three main nutrients that we need to live. Sugars and starches are important sources of energy for both animals and plants.

Our bodies can't break down most kinds of fiber, so we can't use the sugar in fiber for energy. But we do need fiber in our food. It helps keep our digestive system working properly. All three kinds of carbohydrates are important for a strong, healthy body.

THE CARBOHYDRATE FAMILY

Most of the carbohydrates we eat come from plants. Milk and other milk products such as cheese are the only major animal source of carbohydrates in our diet.

Plants make their own carbohydrates, building them in a process called *photosynthesis*. Using energy from sunlight, plants turn carbon dioxide (from the air) and water (from the air and soil) into carbohydrates. Oxygen is left over from this process and is released into the atmosphere. The sunlight energy becomes chemical energy, which is stored in the carbohydrates.

These carbohydrates may be used to build the plant's structure or saved for future energy needs. Animals get carbohydrates mainly by eating plants. Animals also store carbohydrates for future use.

Although carbohydrates can be quite different, they all contain the elements carbon, hydrogen, and oxygen. In most simple sugars, groups of these three chemical elements are arranged to form a ring. These sugar rings can be linked together, much as you link rings of paper strips together to form chains. Simple sugars linked together form the building blocks for more complex carbohydrates such as starches.

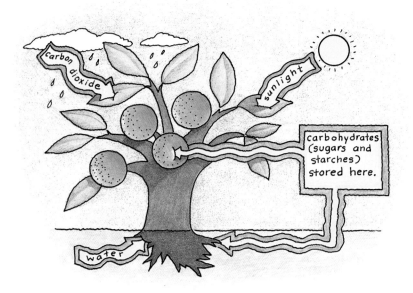

Labels in image: carbon dioxide; sunlight; carbohydrates (sugars and starches) stored here.; water

Simple and Complex Carbohydrates

In simple sugars, each chemical unit—or molecule—contains just a single ring of atoms. *Glucose*, the sugar found in blood, and *fructose*, a sugar in fruits, are simple sugars. Both contain six carbon atoms in each molecule. So do a number of other simple sugars. There are also sugars with smaller or larger numbers of carbon atoms.

Simple sugars are referred to as *monosaccharides*. (*Mono* means "one," and *saccharide* comes from the Latin word for sugar.) Two simple sugars joined together form a *disaccharide*. (*Di* means "two.") A *polysaccharide* is made up of more than two saccharides, and it can contain thousands of these building blocks. (*Poly* means "many.")

Most simple carbohydrates are sweet tasting and dissolve in water. Polysaccharides aren't sweet tasting, and many of them don't dissolve easily in water.

Sugar and starch

Add ½ teaspoon of sugar to 2 ounces of water in a clear glass and stir thoroughly. What happens? (If the sugar "disappears" and the liquid is clear, that means it dissolved.) Now add ½ teaspoon of cornstarch to 2 ounces of water in another clear glass and stir thoroughly. Did the starch dissolve?

Place a drop of the sugar solution on the tip of your tongue. Then rinse your mouth with clear water, and try the same test with a drop of the starch-water (stir it up again first). Which one tastes sweet?

In all the simple sugars, no matter how many carbon atoms they contain, the carbon, hydrogen, and oxygen are in a 1:2:1 ratio—that is, one part carbon, two parts hydrogen, and one part oxygen. But when two simple sugars combine to form a disaccharide, a molecule of water (2 atoms of hydrogen and 1 atom of oxygen) is lost. So the ratios of carbon, hydrogen, and oxygen atoms in disaccharides and other complex carbohydrates are different. (But there are always two hydrogens for each oxygen.)

Simple Sugars

Glucose is the body's most important energy source. This sugar is just mildly sweet, about 70 percent as sweet as table sugar. It is also called *blood sugar*, because it travels in the blood to wherever it is needed in the body. When sold commercially, it is called *dextrose*.

Glucose is the substance that plants produce during photosynthesis. From glucose the plant makes all of the other carbohydrates, including other simple sugars, complex sugars, starches, and cellulose (a fiber).

Fructose is found in fruits and vegetables, such as apples and tomatoes, and it is a very sweet sugar. Why is honey so sweet? The sweetness comes from both glucose and fructose.

Another simple six-carbon sugar is *mannose*, found in apples, oranges, peaches, and the food called manna, as well as in yeast. The five-carbon sugars *ribose* and *deoxyribose* are important parts of *nucleic acids*, which are the "information molecules" of life. Nucleic acids in our chromosomes form the genes, which contain the instructions that make us who we are. Nucleic acids also play an important part in building proteins and producing energy in the body. We don't need to get five-carbon sugars in food; our bodies can make them from other chemicals.

The simple sugars also include some sugar-like substances that don't quite fit the usual 1:2:1 ratio for carbon, hydrogen, and oxygen. *Sugar alcohols*, for example, have a little too much hydrogen. They include some compounds that you may see listed on the labels of chewing gum and other artificially sweetened products: *sorbitol* (from fruits), *mannitol* (from seaweed), and *xylitol* (from berries, wood, or straw). *Sugar acids* have a little extra oxygen. One of the most important sugar acids is *ascorbic acid* (vitamin C). *Amino sugars* contain nitrogen in addition to carbon, hydrogen, and oxygen. Some of them are important building blocks for polysaccharides in animals.

Grow your own rock candy

Note: This activity should be done with the supervision of an adult.

Place ¼ cup of water in a small pot. Place ½ cup of table sugar in a measuring cup. Add a spoonful of the sugar to the water and stir with a wooden spoon until it dissolves. Keep adding sugar until no more will dissolve.

Now heat the mixture gently on a low flame until the rest of the sugar crystals dissolve. Turn off the heat and pour the rest of the sugar into the pot. Heat it gently again, stirring, until all the sugar dissolves and the mixture begins to boil.

Take the mixture off the heat and let it cool for 10 minutes. Then pour out the warm, thick solution into a wide-mouthed jar. Place a popsicle stick in the jar while the liquid is still warm, and allow the jar to cool. Be careful not to bump or shake it.

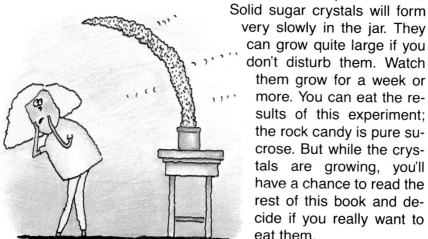

Solid sugar crystals will form very slowly in the jar. They can grow quite large if you don't disturb them. Watch them grow for a week or more. You can eat the results of this experiment; the rock candy is pure sucrose. But while the crystals are growing, you'll have a chance to read the rest of this book and decide if you really want to eat them.

Disaccharides

When you hear the word "sugar," you probably think of the shiny white crystals in your sugar bowl. That sugar is *sucrose*, or table sugar. Each sucrose molecule contains glucose joined with fructose. Sucrose comes from sugarcane and sugar beets. It is very sweet.

Lactose, the sugar in milk, is not very sweet. Each milk sugar molecule contains glucose and another six-carbon sugar, *galactose.*

Two glucose units joined together, form malt sugar, or *maltose.* Cereals and legumes (such as peas and dried beans) contain small amounts of maltose. It is also formed when beer is brewed, and it is used as a flavoring in some candies.

Complex Carbohydrates

Complex carbohydrates are made up of the basic carbohydrate building block: simple sugars. But the sugar units are often linked together in very long chains. Depending on how they are joined together, the same basic units can form quite different complex carbohydrates.

Starch, for example, is made up of thousands of glucose units. There are two main types of carbohydrate chains in starch. In *amylose*, glucose units are joined to form a long, straight chain. In *amylopectin*, the same basic units form a chain with many branches. Plants store starch inside seeds and roots for future energy needs.

Glycogen is the form of carbohydrate that animals store. Sometimes called animal starch, it is also made up of long strings of glucose units, joined in chains with many branches. Our bodies convert glucose to glycogen in the liver and muscles. It can be changed back into glucose when energy is needed.

Cellulose is also made up of many glucose molecules. Together with polysaccharide-like substances called *hemi-*

Storing energy

Generally, plants store more sugars in fruits and more starches in plant seeds, roots, and tubers. The amount of starch and sugar a plant stores depends on the temperature and the amount of moisture in the soil and air where the plant is growing. The amounts of stored sugar and starch can also change. Ripe fruits are sweeter than unripe fruits because some of the stored starch is changed into sugar as a fruit ripens.

celluloses and *pectins*, it forms the structure of plant cell walls. Cellulose is the most common biochemical in the world. More than half of all the carbon in plants is contained in this polysaccharide. Cellulose, hemicelluloses, pectins, and other substances such as mucilages and vegetable gums make up what is called *dietary fiber.*

Chitin, found in the hard outer shells of insects and crabs, is the second most common carbohydrate in the world (after cellulose). It is formed from amino sugar units.

Other Polysaccharides

Dextrins are the polysaccharides that make corn syrup sweet. In the body they are formed when starch is digested.

The slimy stuff on food that has gone moldy is another type of polysaccharide, *dextrans*. It is made by bacteria and yeast. *Dextrans* that are produced by bacteria living in the mouth help to form deposits called plaque. Bacteria living in the plaque change carbohydrates into acids that eat away tooth enamel, forming cavities.

In *mucopolysaccharides*, amino sugars are combined with sugar acids or simple sugars. *Heparin*, which keeps blood from clotting, belongs to this group. Sugars may also be attached to proteins or fats. *Mucin*, for example, is a sugar-containing protein that makes saliva slippery.

CARBOHYDRATES IN FOODS

When we think of carbohydrates, we usually think of starchy foods such as spaghetti, potatoes, rice, cereal, or bread, or sugary foods like candy, cookies, and ice cream. But many other foods are high in carbohydrates too—fruits and vegetables, for example.

You'd probably be surprised to find out how much carbohydrate there is in some foods. A 12-ounce can of cola, for example, contains as much carbohydrate as nine teaspoons of sugar or three slices of bread!

Carbohydrates are the main source of food energy for people all over the world. In the United States, about 40 to 50 percent of our calories come from carbohydrates. But in some countries, carbohydrates make up as much as 80 or even 90 percent of the total calories. In Asia, for example, rice is one of the main foods. In eastern Europe bread is a major part of the diet, and in Britain and Ireland people eat a lot of potatoes.

Why are carbohydrates so popular?

In general, they cost less than proteins. Carbohydrate-rich foods are easier to store, too, because they don't spoil as easily as fat-rich and protein-rich foods.

Carbohydrate foods are appealing because of their flavor, color, and texture. They also taste good. Most people enjoy some kind of carbohydrate with every meal, because eating just protein and fat is not satisfying.

Energy Foods

The energy in food is stored in the form of chemical bonds between atoms. This chemical energy can be freed by combining the foods with oxygen from the air, just as oxygen combines with materials when they are burned in a fire. The energy that is released is measured in units called calories. And this energy can be used to do work—for example, providing the fuel for the body's chemical reactions.

Most people think carbohydrates are very high in calories. Actually, a gram of carbohydrate contains about 4 calories of stored energy—about the same amount as there is in a gram of protein. (But our bodies normally use proteins for building materials instead of burning them to produce energy.) Fats are a more concentrated energy storehouse: A gram of fat contains nine calories of stored energy—more than twice as much as either carbohydrate or protein.

Package labels usually give the amounts of carbohydrates, fats, and proteins in grams. But it is easy to figure out the percentage of carbohydrate calories. Just multiply the carbohydrate grams by four, divide that answer by the total calories per portion, and multiply by 100.

How much carbohydrate?

A box of cornflakes says that a 1-ounce serving contains:

	Cereal (1 ounce)	Cereal with 1/2 cup skim milk
Calories	110	150
Protein	2 g	6 g
Carbohydrate	24 g	30 g
Starch	22 g	22 g
Sugar	2 g	8 g
Fat	0 g	0 g

How does your favorite cereal compare?

Note: Experts recommend eating cereals with no more than 6 grams of sugar per serving.

What Are Empty Calories?

Most carbohydrate-rich foods contain many other nutrients, too. Potatoes, rice, corn, and bread, for example, supply protein, vitamins, and minerals along with their complex carbohydrates.

But foods that are high in sugars usually don't contain many other nutrients. Table sugar, honey, and syrup are almost pure carbohydrate. Foods that have a lot of calories without supplying much of any other nutrients are said to contain "empty calories." A baked potato and 8 ounces of

soda both have about 100 calories, but the potato is loaded with vitamins, minerals, and even some protein; the soda only has sugar.

The Sweet Taste of Food

If you have a "sweet tooth," you are not unusual. Although foods with complex carbohydrates are generally better for us than foods high in sugars, most people enjoy foods that taste sweet.

People use sugar in cooking and baking. Many also add sugar at the table—on cereals, in tea, and on a grapefruit, for example.

Even if you don't add sugar to foods, and don't eat empty-calorie sweets like candy, you're probably still eating a lot more sugar than you think. The average person eats about 36 teaspoons of sugar each day—about 130 pounds a year! Most of that sugar (70 percent) is hidden in foods you might not suspect, such as cereals, ketchup, peanut butter, and sodas.

Be a smart label reader

Most ingredient labels just list the grams for "carbohydrates" and don't say how much of that total is sugar and how much is starch. So it's hard to tell exactly how much sugar you are eating. But there is some other information on the label that can give you a good idea.

Ingredients are listed in order, from the largest amounts down to the smallest. So if sugar is close to the beginning of the list of ingredients, you know there is a lot of sugar in the food.

Check some ingredient labels on foods around the house. Some foods have three or four different sugary sweeteners added, and they may be hiding under some unexpected names.

For example:

brown sugar	lactose
corn sweetener	maltose
corn syrup	mannitol
dextrose	maple syrup
fructose	molasses
fruit juice	raw sugar
concentrate	sorbitol
glucose	sucrose
honey	sugar
high fructose	syrup
corn syrup	table sugar

Artificial Sweeteners

Many people trying to watch their weight don't want the calories in sugar, but they still like the sweet taste that sugar offers. There are several substitutes that can be used to provide a sweet taste.

Saccharin is a common sweetener found in diet sodas, candies, and gums. It is a manufactured chemical, not a food substance, and it has no calories at all. Scientists discovered saccharin's sweetness (500 times as sweet as sugar!) by accident and named it after the sugars. (Remember the mono-, di-, and poly*sacchar*ides?) Although saccharin tastes very sweet at first, it leaves a bitter aftertaste.

How sweet is it?

Here's how some other sugars and sweeteners compare with sucrose:

Sucrose = 100%

Not as sweet		Sweeter	
Glucose	75%	Saccharin	50,000%
Corn syrup	60%	Aspartame	18,000%
Sorbitol	60%	Fructose	170%
Mannitol	50%	Honey	120–170%
Galactose	32%	Molasses	110%
Maltose	32%		
Lactose	16%		

Aspartame (Nutrasweet) is used in soft drinks, candies, puddings, dessert toppings, and cereals. (You can't bake with it, though, because it breaks down when heated.) Aspartame is made from two amino acids. (Amino acids are the building blocks of proteins.) It is so much sweeter than sugar that you need much less of it. Just a tenth of a calorie of aspartame provides as much sweetness as a teaspoon of sugar. This sweetener has a sugar-like taste, without any bitter aftertaste.

Sorbitol and mannitol, used in sugarless gums, are sugar substitutes, but they aren't calorie-free. They actually have as many calories as sugar. But they supposedly don't promote cavities the way sugar can.

Complex Carbohydrates

Fruits usually contain more sugars than starches. Grains, nuts, legumes, root vegetables, and potatoes are good sources of starch. Most (70 to 80 percent) of the solid material in bread and cereals is starch!

Processing foods can change the carbohydrates they contain. When dry cereals are made or when bread is baked, the heat changes some of the starch into dextrins. Some starches, particularly in cereals, are broken down even further into maltose.

Fiber

The fiber in foods doesn't supply any calories because we can't use these complex carbohydrates. Their glucose units

Why do we cook starchy foods?

Note: Cooking activities should be done under the supervision of an adult. You can eat the rice when you are finished.

The starch in plants is held inside the plant cell walls, which don't dissolve in water. During cooking, the tiny starch grains absorb water and swell up. They get so big that the cell walls burst. Then the starch is easier to digest.

You can see for yourself how much water starchy foods can hold. Pour out 1/3 cup of dry rice and weigh it on a diet scale. Then put 1 cup of water in a small pot and heat it until it starts to boil. Turn the flame down to "low" and add the rice. Continue to heat the mixture, stirring every few minutes, until all the water disappears.

Carefully scoop out the rice into a measuring cup. How much is there now? Weigh the cooked rice on a diet scale. How much weight did it gain? All that is absorbed water.

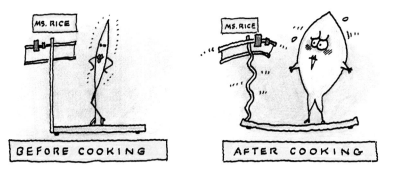

are joined in such a way that our digestive enzymes can't break the bonds holding them together. (Enzymes are proteins that help other chemicals react.)

There are many different types of fiber, even some that are water soluble (will dissolve in water). They all have different jobs in the body. Eating a wide variety of foods helps you to get all the kinds of fiber.

The major insoluble fibers (those that don't dissolve in water) are *cellulose* and *hemicellulose*. Cellulose and hemicellulose are found in plant cell walls. (Cotton balls are nearly pure cellulose.) In whole grains these two types of fiber are found in the *bran* layer, the protective outer covering over the starchy part. They are also found in seeds and the skins of fruits and vegetables.

The other main type of fiber is soluble in water. *Pectins* and *gums* are soluble fibers. Apples and citrus fruits have a lot of pectin. Most plants usually only have small amounts

Did you know . . .

People don't eat grass because we can't digest the cellulose in the plant cell walls. So we can't get any nourishment from the complex carbohydrates grass contains. But rabbits, cows, sheep, horses, and goats do eat grass. Yet their bodies don't make cellulose-digesting enzymes, either. How can they live on their plant diet? They have help. Bacteria that live in their digestive systems break down the cellulose in their food, allowing the animals to use the digested material for energy.

of gums. Pectins are used as food additives to thicken many foods or to give them a jelly-like texture. Guar gum and locust bean gum are also used as food additives.

Eating the "whole" thing . . .

When you peel and core an apple, you are throwing away a lot of fiber. An apple with its peel has about 3.6 grams of fiber. A half cup of applesauce has 2.1 grams of fiber, and ³/₄ cup of apple juice has only 0.2 gram of fiber—less than ten percent of the fiber of a whole apple!

Other "throwaway" food fibers include the bran of wheat and other grains, removed in making flour, and rice bran, removed from white rice. (White rice and "enriched flour" have some vitamins and other nutrients added. But not all of the nutrients that were in the original whole grain are replaced.)

Fiber is now being added to many products—for example, bran in cereals and breads. Some people even take fiber supplements, such as bran (mainly insoluble fiber) and psyllium (a soluble fiber).

Sometimes package labels list the amount of dietary fiber. But those numbers are only a rough estimate. It is hard to measure and calculate all the different kinds of fiber in foods. You can get a better idea of how much fiber foods provide by looking for some key fiber names.

Look on labels for whole-grain ingredients—those that are more like the natural grains. Whole-grain foods include bulgur, brown rice, oatmeal, popcorn, scotch rye, whole cornmeal, whole rye, and whole wheat.

WHAT HAPPENS TO THE FOOD YOU EAT?

The organs of the digestive system are like work stations in a factory. Step by step, they prepare food for digestion, break down the nutrients into forms the body can use, and get rid of waste products.

Did you know . . .

Digestion can start when you smell food or even think about it, before you eat anything. Picture a tray of fresh-baked cookies, a thick, juicy steak, a ripe apple, or your own favorite food. Can you feel the watery saliva flowing into your mouth?

You can prove for yourself that saliva helps digest complex carbohydrates. Bite off a large piece of a plain soda cracker and start chewing it. Keep on chewing, without swallowing, much longer than you normally would. Soon the starchy cracker will taste sweet.

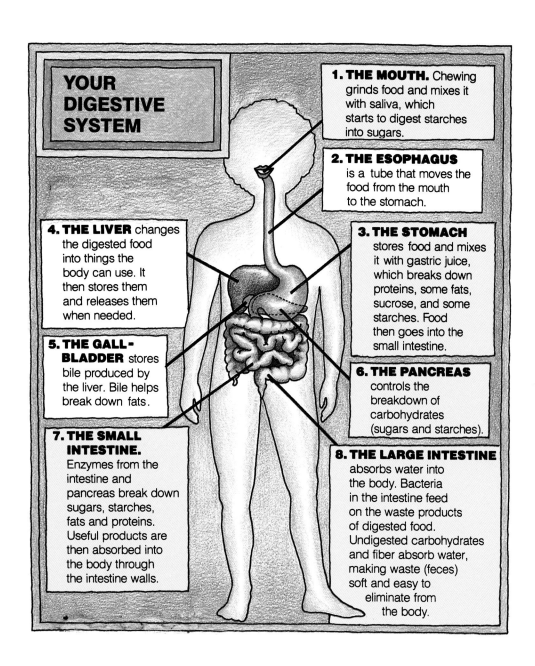

YOUR DIGESTIVE SYSTEM

1. THE MOUTH. Chewing grinds food and mixes it with saliva, which starts to digest starches into sugars.

2. THE ESOPHAGUS is a tube that moves the food from the mouth to the stomach.

4. THE LIVER changes the digested food into things the body can use. It then stores them and releases them when needed.

3. THE STOMACH stores food and mixes it with gastric juice, which breaks down proteins, some fats, sucrose, and some starches. Food then goes into the small intestine.

5. THE GALL-BLADDER stores bile produced by the liver. Bile helps break down fats.

6. THE PANCREAS controls the breakdown of carbohydrates (sugars and starches).

7. THE SMALL INTESTINE. Enzymes from the intestine and pancreas break down sugars, starches, fats and proteins. Useful products are then absorbed into the body through the intestine walls.

8. THE LARGE INTESTINE absorbs water into the body. Bacteria in the intestine feed on the waste products of digested food. Undigested carbohydrates and fiber absorb water, making waste (feces) soft and easy to eliminate from the body.

29)

Quick energy

The simple sugars in food don't have to be digested, and disaccharides such as sucrose are digested very quickly. If you eat some table sugar, the glucose level in your blood will increase in just a few minutes. More complex carbohydrates will raise the blood sugar level in less than an hour.

What happens to the carbohydrates we can't digest?

Bacteria living in the large intestine can break down some of the carbohydrates that we can't. But they may produce gas as a by-product. Undigested carbohydrates also soak up water. Too much causes diarrhea. Some people get cramps, gas, and diarrhea when they eat milk or dairy products. The reason is that they can't digest lactose (milk sugar). Many adults have this problem, called *lactose intolerance.*

CARBOHYDRATES IN THE BODY

In plants, carbohydrates of many different kinds are the building materials that form the plant structures. In animals—like you—proteins are the body's main structural materials. Carbohydrates have a different but equally important job: providing energy.

Fuel for the Body

In the last chapter we saw how carbohydrates in foods are digested and broken down into glucose. This simple sugar is the body's main energy source. It is carried in the bloodstream throughout the body, so that energy is available to any cell that needs it. Muscle cells use a lot of glucose. These cells work hard whenever you move a body part—when you walk or run, pick up a package, or throw a ball. Your heart is also a muscle, which pumps the blood that flows through your body. Your brain and nerves are big glucose users, too. Did you know it takes energy to think?

How does the body get energy out of glucose? It uses the chemical reactions of *respiration*. Do you remember that plants use sunlight energy in photosynthesis to put carbon dioxide and water together, forming glucose and producing oxygen as a by-product? Respiration is just the opposite. When glucose and oxygen react, chemical bonds are broken, carbon dioxide and water are formed, and energy is released.

Keeping Blood Sugar Levels Normal

It is important to keep enough glucose in the blood so that this energy source will always be available to the body's cells. But too much sugar in the blood can cause problems. So the body needs to keep the amount of sugar in the blood fairly constant.

Keeping the body's blood sugar level within a normal range is a complicated juggling act. After a meal, when extra glucose is entering the blood, the liver takes some sugar out and stores it in the form of the animal starch called glycogen. Then, when we haven't eaten in a while and body cells have been using up glucose from the blood, the liver breaks down some of its stored glycogen into glucose, which passes into the blood. The liver also changes part of the glucose it picks up to fats.

Several hormones (chemical messengers that travel in the bloodstream) help to coordinate all these glucose-regulating activities. When the blood sugar level rises, the pancreas sends *insulin* into the blood. This hormone works to lower the blood sugar level. *Glucagon*, also produced in

the pancreas, and *glucocorticoids* from the adrenal glands help raise the blood sugar level when it falls too low. Another adrenal hormone, *adrenaline*, is called the "fight or flight" hormone. It helps provide extra energy for emergencies by telling the liver to break down glycogen and put more glucose into the blood. The thyroid hormone *thyroxin* speeds up the body's use of energy.

When Things Go Wrong

Some people can't handle carbohydrates the way they're supposed to. Perhaps the pancreas doesn't produce enough insulin, or this hormone doesn't work properly. Then the cells don't take glucose out of the blood. The blood sugar level rises as glucose from digested foods continues to enter the bloodstream. Some of the excess glucose is removed when the blood flows through the kidneys.

This blood sugar problem, called *diabetes mellitus*, can be very serious. Many important body reactions are

upset. If the pancreas is not producing enough insulin,
injections of this hormone can keep a diabetic's blood
sugar at the right level. Exercise and a diet higher in fiber
and lower in calories can help in some types of diabetes.
There are also drugs that lower the blood sugar level.

In some people, the pancreas sends out too much insulin after a high-carbohydrate meal. The blood sugar falls
too low (*hypoglycemia*), and the body's cells don't get
enough glucose. The person may feel very tired or may
even faint. Eating smaller, more frequent meals, low in
sugar and high in proteins and complex carbohydrates, can
help.

Some Carbohydrates Form Body Structures

Some carbohydrates help to build structural parts in the
bones, skin, nails, and cartilage. Sugar proteins linked into
a fine mesh give structure to the jelly-like substance that
fills the eyeballs. Sugar fats are important parts of the brain
and spinal cord. And the body can use sugars to make
some of the amino acid building blocks of proteins.

(34

CARBOHYDRATES AND GOOD HEALTH

People have blamed sugary foods like candies and soft drinks for many health problems, including acne, anemia, cancer, hyperactivity, high blood pressure, heart disease, and kidney failure. But none of these claims have been proved in medical studies.

There is one health area where carbohydrates (sugars, in particular) do deserve their bad reputation: tooth decay. Cavities develop when the enamel on a tooth is worn away by acids produced by bacteria. These bacteria live in the mouth and feed on sugars from foods.

Some kinds of sugary foods seem to cause more problems than others. Caramels and raisins, for example, stick to teeth and provide food and shelter for the bacteria that cause decay. Sugary foods eaten with meals are less likely to cause tooth decay than those eaten as snacks between meals. Babies sometimes develop cavities when they go to sleep drinking a bottle of milk or juice.

Eating too many sugary foods can also lead to malnutrition. The empty calories make people feel too full to want to eat more nutritious foods. Or they may be so used to eating sweet-tasting things that vegetables and other

Carbohydrates and athletes

Athletes sometimes use "carbohydrate loading" to help them perform better. By changing the amount of exercise and eating extra carbohydrates for several days before an athletic event, they can get their muscles to store up extra glycogen. With this extra fuel supply, their muscles can keep working longer without getting tired—which may make a difference, for example, in a long-distance race.

Carbohydrate loading isn't something to fool around with by yourself, though. In fact, this kind of change in the body's normal workings can actually put dangerous stress on a child's or adolescent's health.

nutrient-packed foods don't taste good to them. Eventually these people may develop health problems because they're not getting enough of some vitamins, minerals, or protein.

Can Carbohydrates Make You Fat?

Can starchy foods like bread, rice, potatoes, and spaghetti make you fat? Many people think so, and it is true that any extra carbohydrates that the body doesn't need will be converted into fat. But carbohydrates actually have less than half the calories of fats. So you can feel full without eating as many calories. Many starchy foods also contain fiber, which helps you feel full without any calories.

Sugary foods are often fatty foods, too. Cake, cookies, candy, and ice cream, for example, may be high in both sugar and fat, which increases the calories even more. Eating too many calories of any kind can contribute to obesity (being severely overweight), and this increases your risk for some forms of cancer, heart disease, and many other health problems for which carbohydrates have been blamed.

Fiber: The Wonder Food

Americans don't eat enough fiber. Most people eat 10 to 20 grams of fiber a day, only half of the recommended amount. Doctors believe this is one reason that many people suffer from digestive problems.

Fiber helps keep people regular by absorbing water and making the feces soft and bulky, which keeps things moving through the system properly. So eating more fiber can help people who suffer from constipation.

Researchers believe that some kinds of fiber can help reduce the chances of colon cancer and heart disease by carrying harmful substances out of the body quickly, before they have time to do damage. Dietary fiber binds to cholesterol and carries it out of the body, so a high-fiber diet may help to lower cholesterol levels, too.

Eating Right

Health experts suggest that 55 percent of all your calories should come from carbohydrates, 15 percent from proteins, and no more than 30 percent from fats. To reach those goals, most Americans need to eat less fatty foods, less sugars, more complex carbohydrates, and more fiber.

Do you know what you're eating?

How many total calories do these meals supply? What is the percentage of carbohydrate calories in each meal? (Use the chart of food values on pages 40–41 to figure it out.)

Orange juice, cornflakes with milk and banana, milk.

Bacon and eggs, toast (white bread), milk.

Peanut butter and jelly sandwich, milk.

Tuna salad with celery and salad dressing, lettuce and tomato, milk.

Hamburger on a bun with ketchup and onions, french fries, milkshake.

Steak, baked potato, green beans, lettuce and tomatoes, chocolate ice cream.

Broiled cod, corn, broccoli, roll and butter, applesauce, milk.

Spaghetti with tomato sauce, eggplant, broccoli, peaches, tea.

Turkey, stuffing, cranberries, sweet potatoes, peas, pumpkin pie, milk.

Eating the right foods in the right amounts helps young, growing bodies stay healthy. By knowing the nutritional values of the foods you eat, you can help make sure your body gets everything it needs.

Nutritional Values of Common Foods

Food	Portion size		Total calories	Carbohydrates (grams)	Carbohydrates (calories)
Applesauce (sweetened)	1	cup	195	51.0	190
Bacon	3	pieces	109	traces	traces
Banana	1	banana	105	26.7	95
Broccoli (raw)	1	cup	24	4.6	10
Bun (hamburger)	1	bun	114	20.1	80
Butter	1	tablespoon	108	0.0	0
Cake (devil's food)	1	piece	227	30.4	122
Celery	1/2	cup	10	2.6	8
Cod (baked w/butter)	3 1/2	ounces	132	0.0	0
Cookies (choc. chip)	2	cookies	99	16.0	64
Corn (cooked on cob)	1	ear	83	19.0	62
Cornflakes	1 1/4	cups	110	25.0	100
Cranberry sauce (jellied)	1/2	cup	209	53.7	206
Eggplant (boiled)	1/2	cup	13	3.2	10
Eggs (boiled)	1	large	79	1.0	4
French fries	10	fries	158	20.0	75
Green beans (boiled)	1/2	cup	22	5.0	15
Hamburger (broiled)	3 1/2	ounces	289	0.0	0
Hot dog (beef)	1	frank	142	0.8	3
Ice cream (chocolate)	1/2	cup	280	25.0	100
Jelly	1	tablespoon	49	12.7	49
Ketchup	1	tablespoon	16	3.8	14
Lettuce (iceberg)	1	cup	7	1.0	4
Milk (whole)	1	cup	150	11.0	44

Nutritional Values of Common Foods

Food	Portion size		Total calories	Carbohydrates (grams)	Carbohydrates (calories)
Milkshake (chocolate)	1	cup	230	28.0	112
Onions (raw)	½	cup	27	5.9	21
Orange juice	1	cup	111	26.0	100
Peaches	1	peach	37	9.7	34
Peanut butter	1	tablespoon	95	2.5	3
Peas (boiled)	½	cup	67	12.5	48
Potato (baked w/peel)	1	potato	220	51.0	198
Pumpkin pie	1	piece	367	51.0	187
Roll (dinner)	1	roll	85	14.0	56
Salad dressing (mayo.)	1	tablespoon	57	3.5	13
Spaghetti	1	cup	159	33.7	132
Steak (sirloin)	3	ounces	240	0.0	0
Stuffing (bread)	1	cup	416	39.4	158
Sweet potatoes (baked)	1	potato	118	28.0	109
Tea	1	cup	2	0.4	2
Toast (white bread)	1	slice	64	11.7	47
Tomatoes	1	tomato	24	5.3	17
Tomato juice	1	cup	48	10.2	42
Tomato sauce	½	cup	37	8.8	29
Tuna (in water)	3	ounces	111	0.0	0
Tuna (in oil)	3	ounces	169	0.0	0
Turkey (light meat)	3½	ounces	157	0.0	0

Note: Grams of carbohydrates include sugar, starch, and fiber.

GLOSSARY

amylopectin and *amylose*—polysaccharides that form starch.

ascorbic acid—vitamin C (a sugar acid).

blood sugar level—the amount of glucose in the blood.

bran—the outer covering of a grain.

cellulose—a polysaccharide of glucose units that humans cannot digest; the main component of plant cell walls.

chitin—a polysaccharide found in the hard outer shell of insects.

deoxyribose—a simple sugar found in DNA, which carries the hereditary information in the genes.

dextrans—polysaccharides produced by tooth decay bacteria.

diabetes mellitus—a disease in which the body cannot keep the blood sugar level under control.

dietary fiber—indigestible plant substances including the polysaccharides cellulose, hemicelluloses, and pectins.

disaccharide—two simple sugars joined together.

fructose—a simple sugar found in fruits.

galactose—a simple sugar; part of lactose (milk sugar).

glucagon—a hormone that raises the blood sugar level.

glucocorticoids—hormones that help raise the blood sugar level.

glucose—a simple sugar found in blood.

glycogen—a polysaccharide of glucose units found in animals.

insulin—a hormone that lowers the blood sugar level.

lactose—a disaccharide found in milk.

maltose—a disaccharide, malt sugar.

monosaccharides—simple sugars.

mucopolysaccharides—combinations containing amino sugars.

photosynthesis—the production of carbohydrates by plants from carbon dioxide and water, using energy from sunlight.

polysaccharides—carbohydrates containing more than two simple sugar units.

respiration—the reaction of glucose with oxygen, releasing stored energy.

ribose—a simple sugar found in RNA, which helps to build proteins.

starch—a polysaccharide of glucose units.

sucrose—a disaccharide, table sugar.

FOR FURTHER READING

Cobb, Vicki. *More Science Experiments You Can Eat.* New York: Lippincott, 1979.

Cobb, Vicki. *Science Experiments You Can Eat.* New York: Lippincott, 1972.

O'Neill, Catherine. *How and Why: A Kid's Book About the Body.* Mount Vernon, N.Y.: Consumer Reports Books, 1988.

Ontario Science Center. *Foodworks.* Toronto: Kids Can Press, 1986.

Our Body: A Child's First Library of Learning. Alexandria, Va.: Time Life Books, 1988.

INDEX